This coloring book belongs to

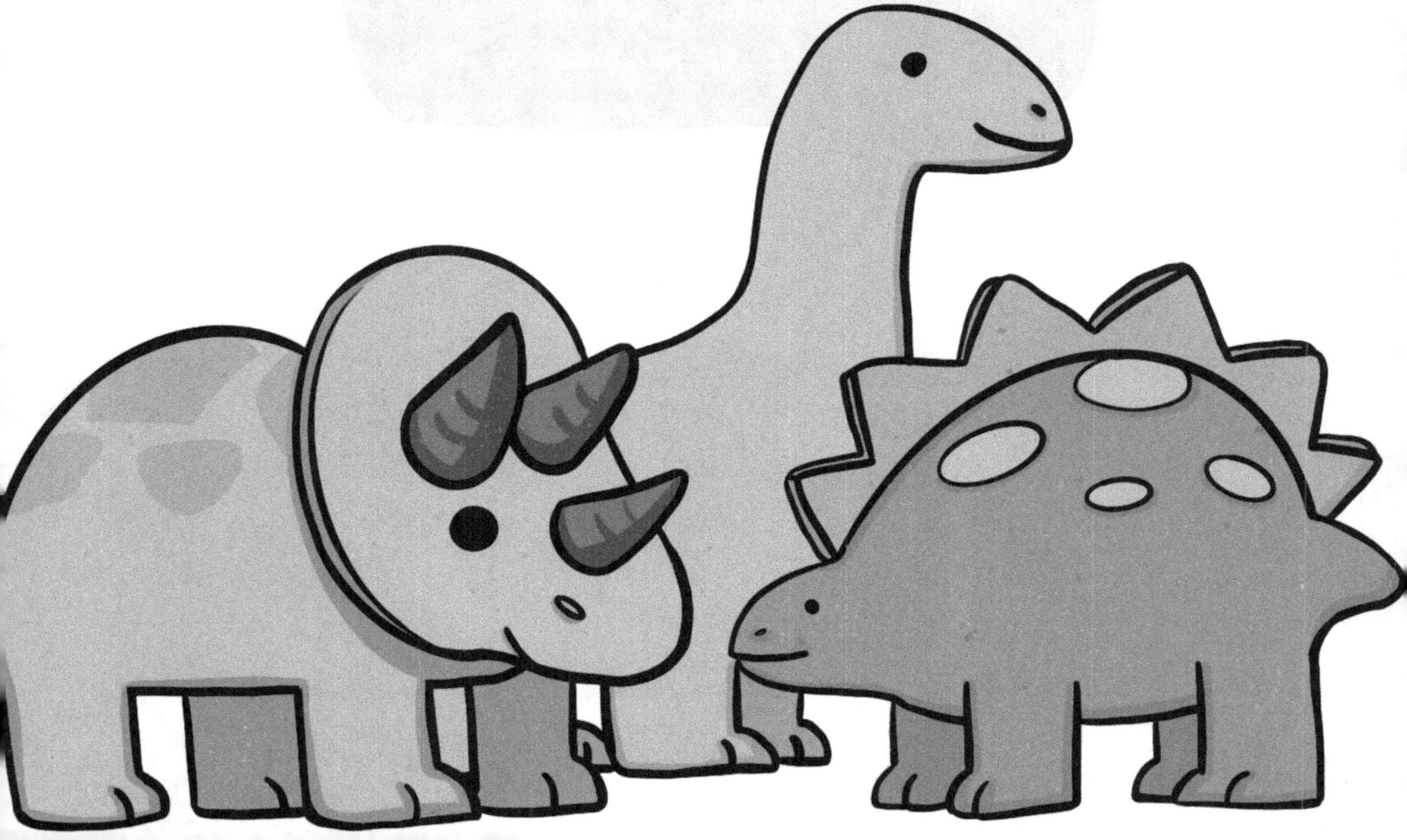

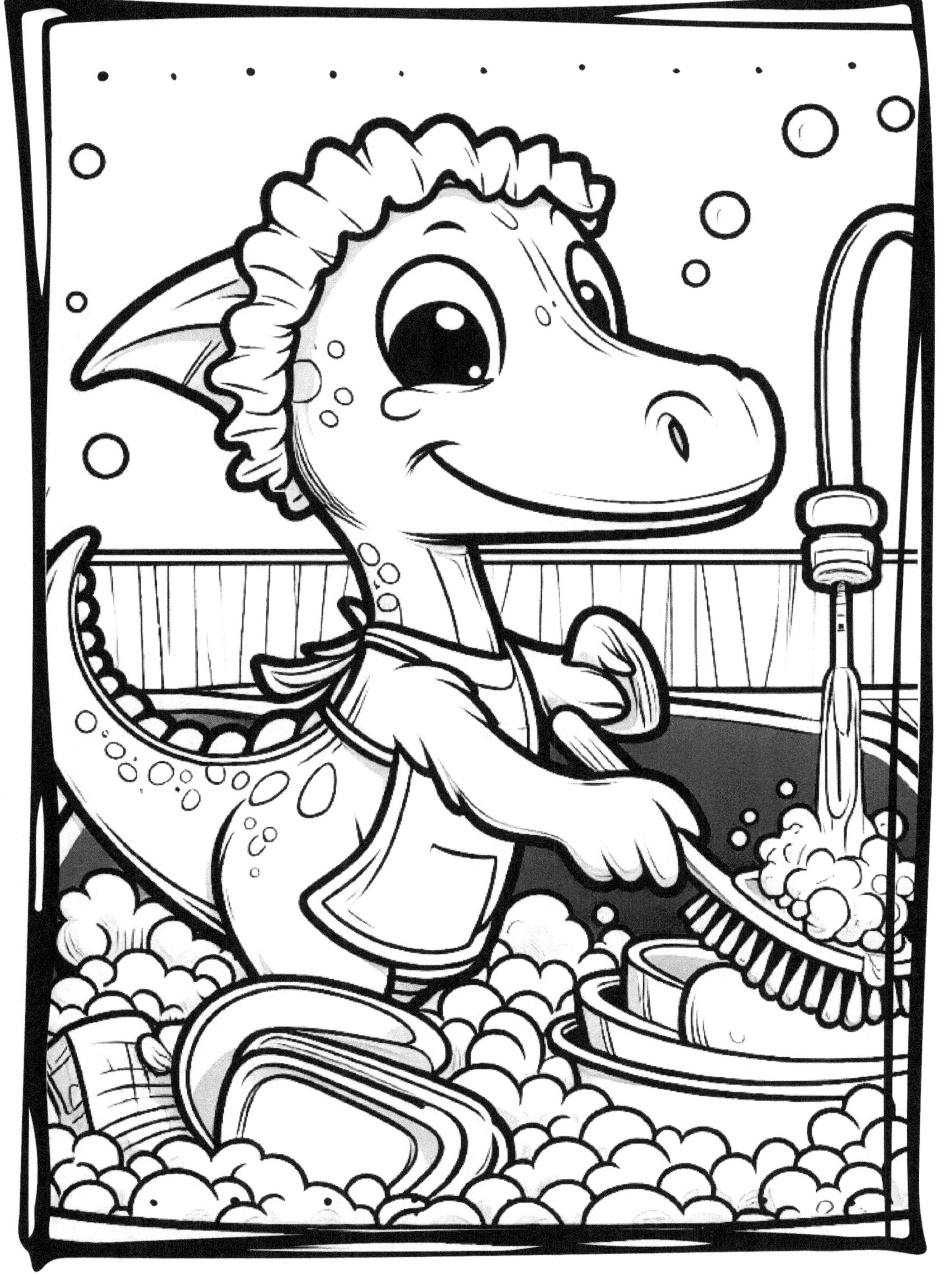

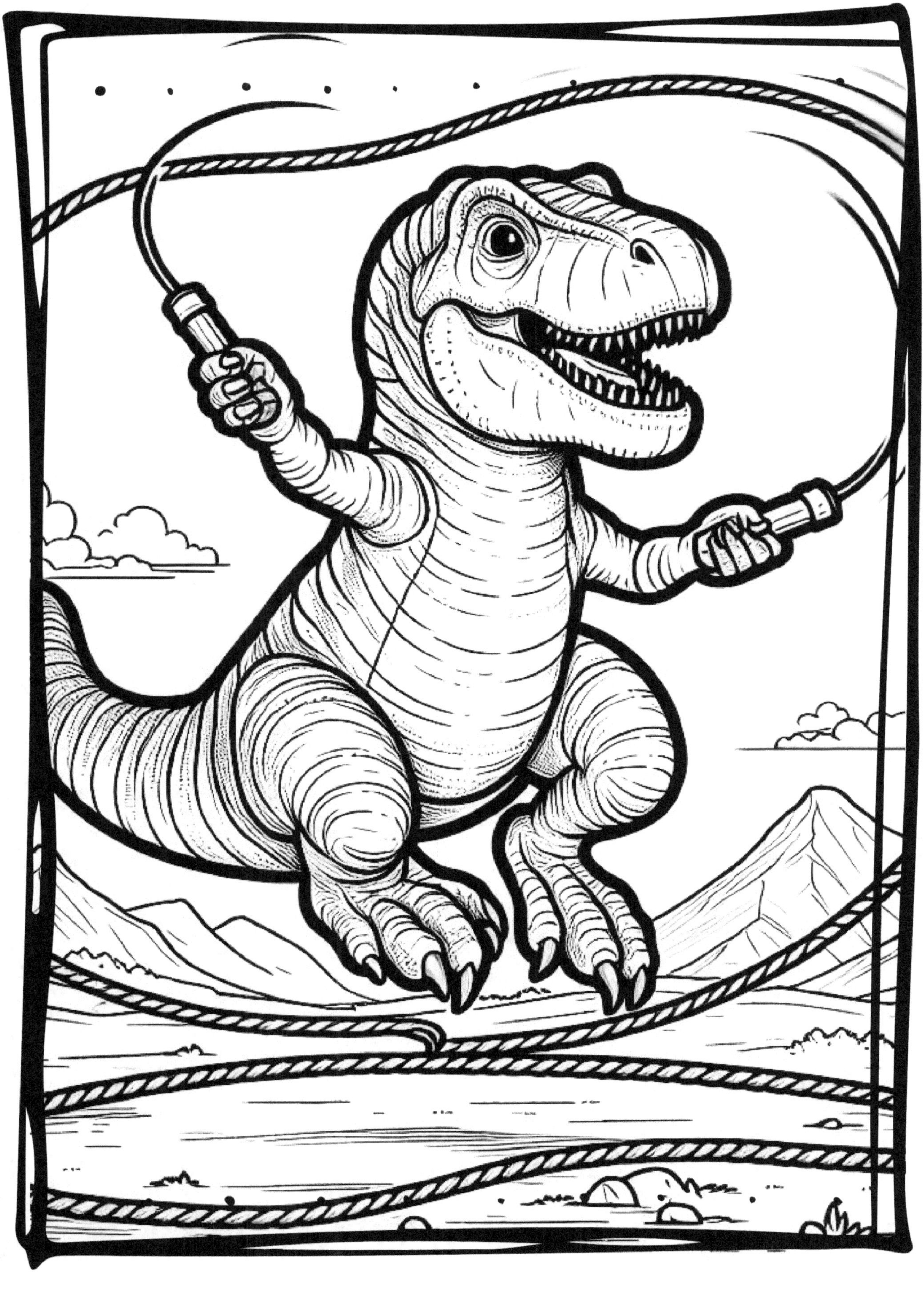

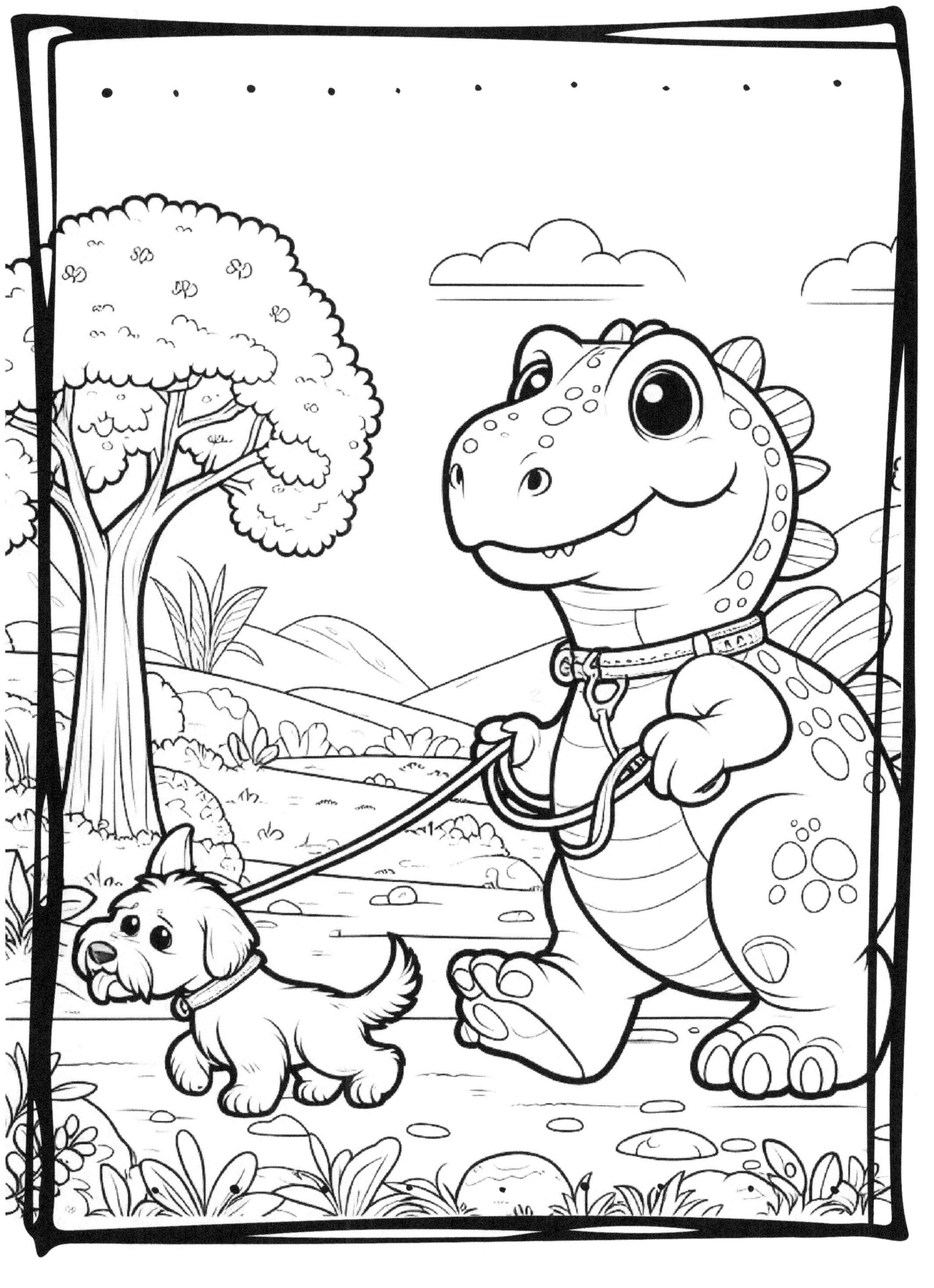

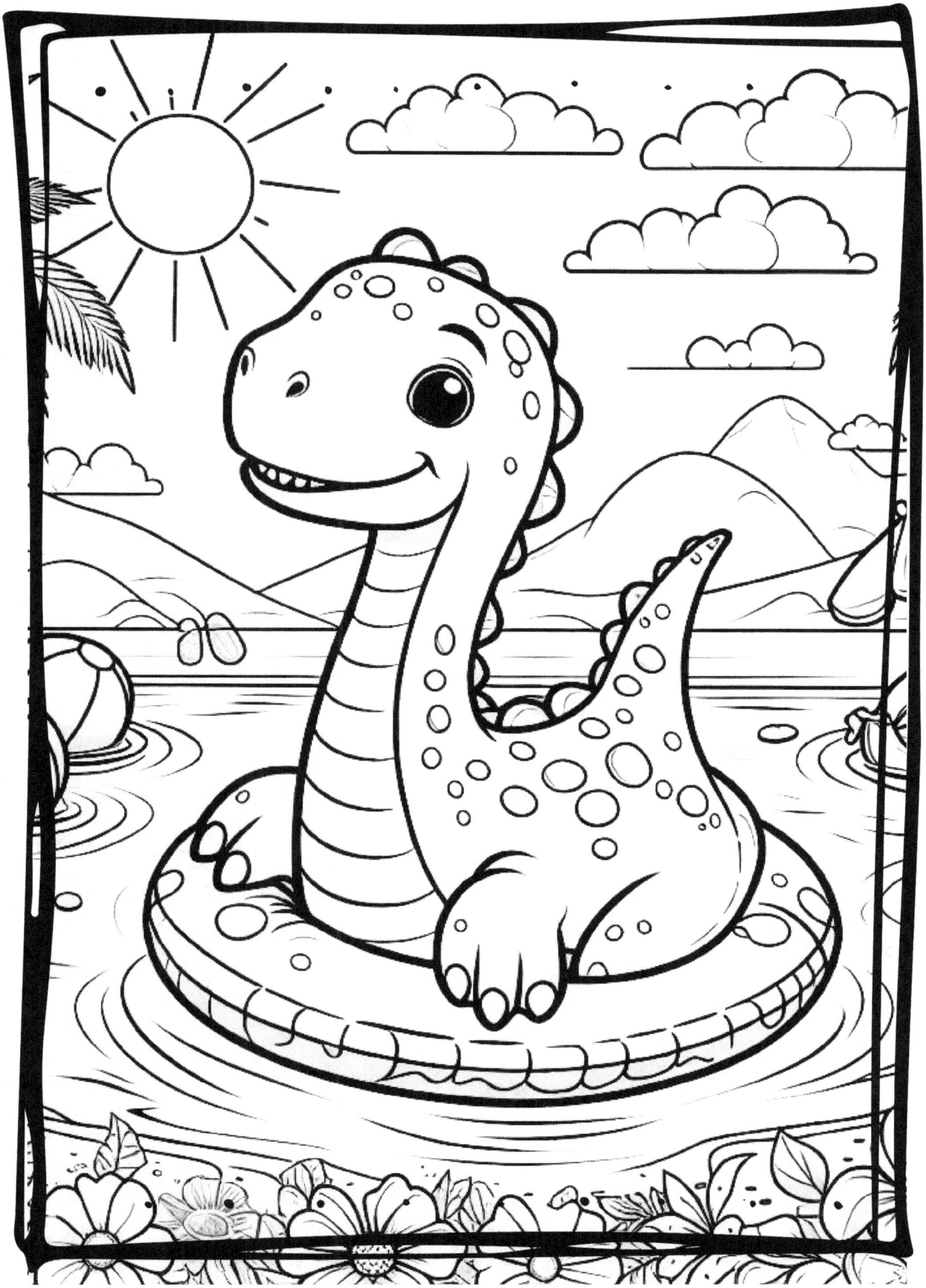

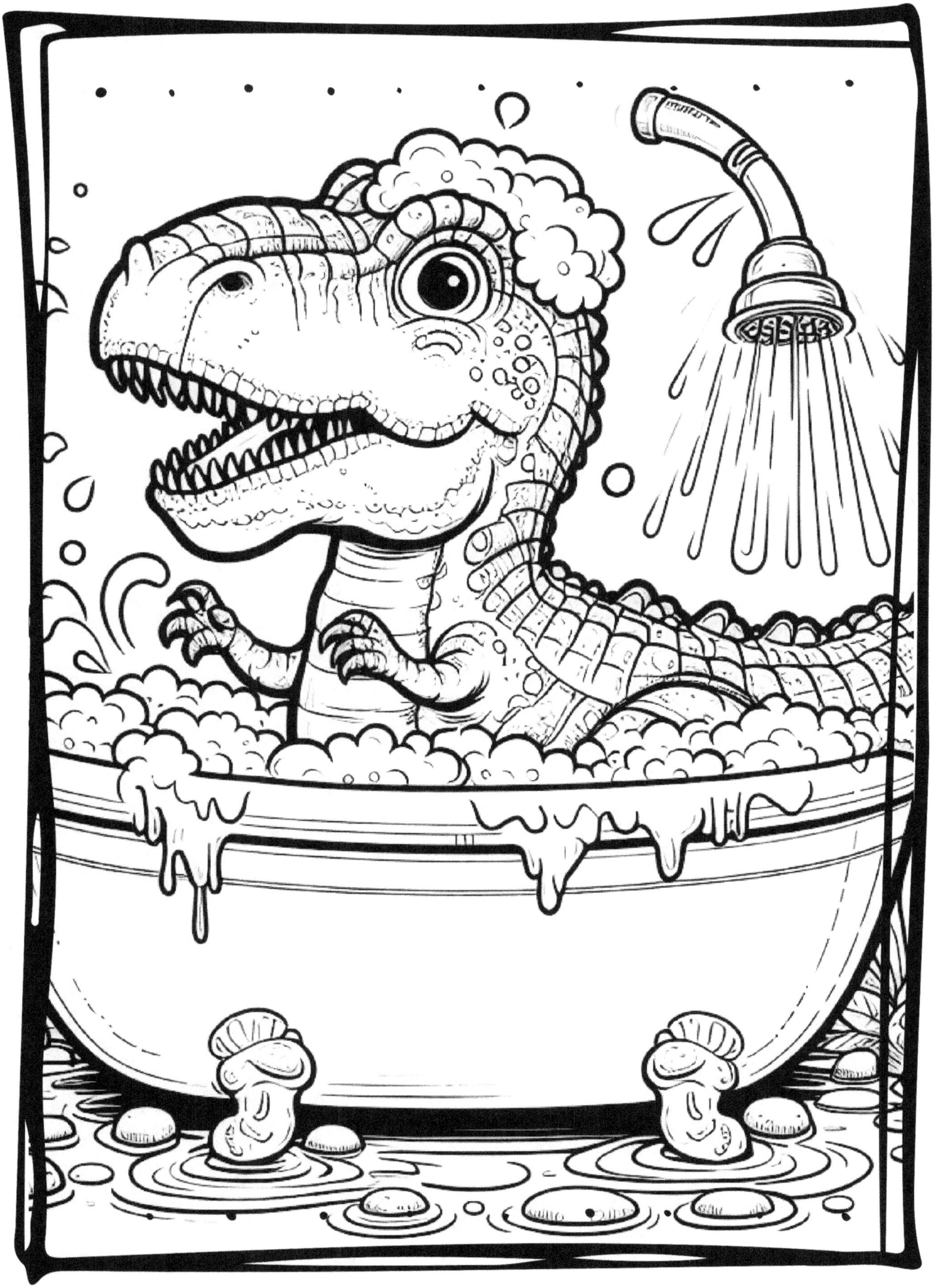

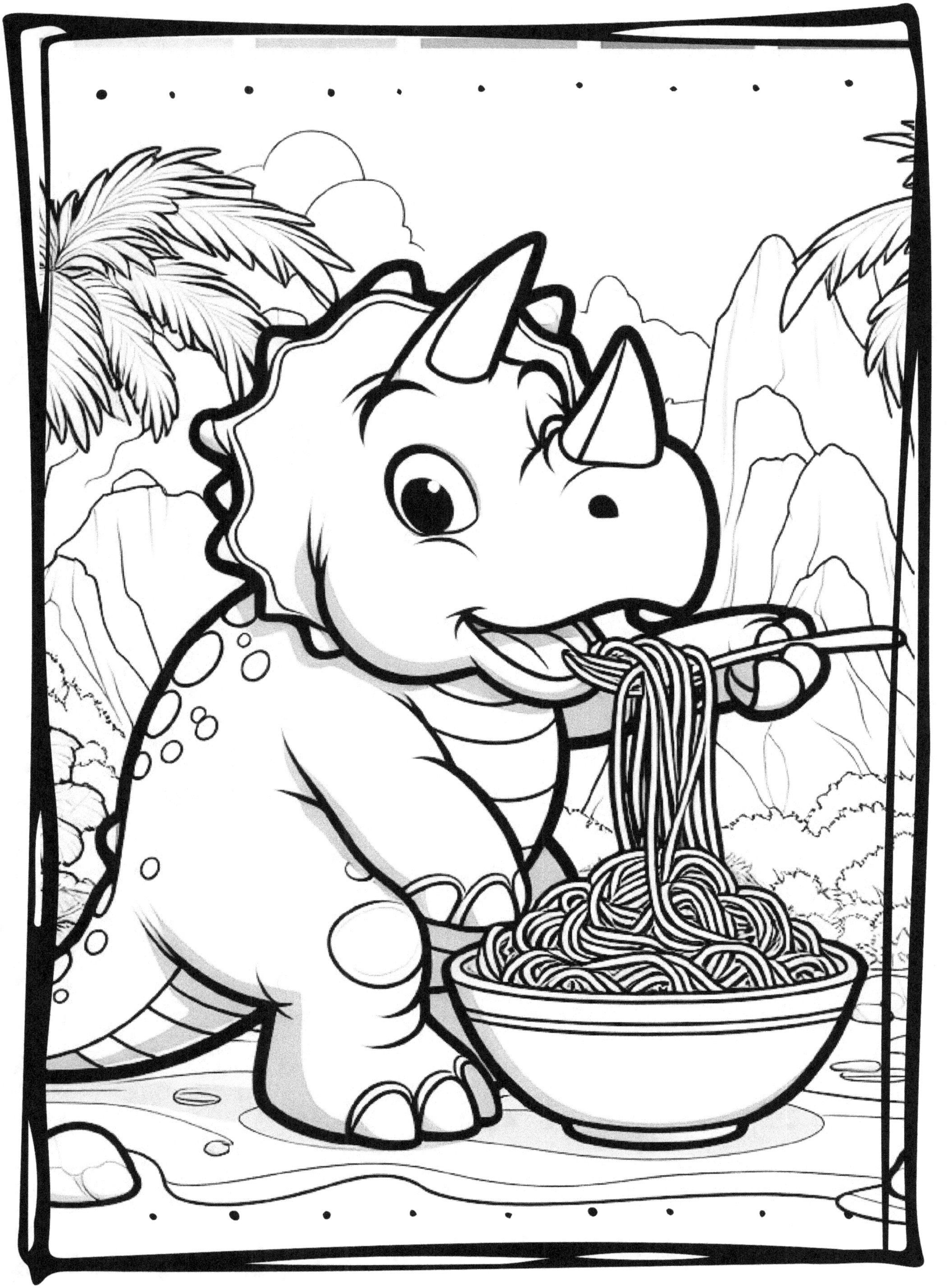

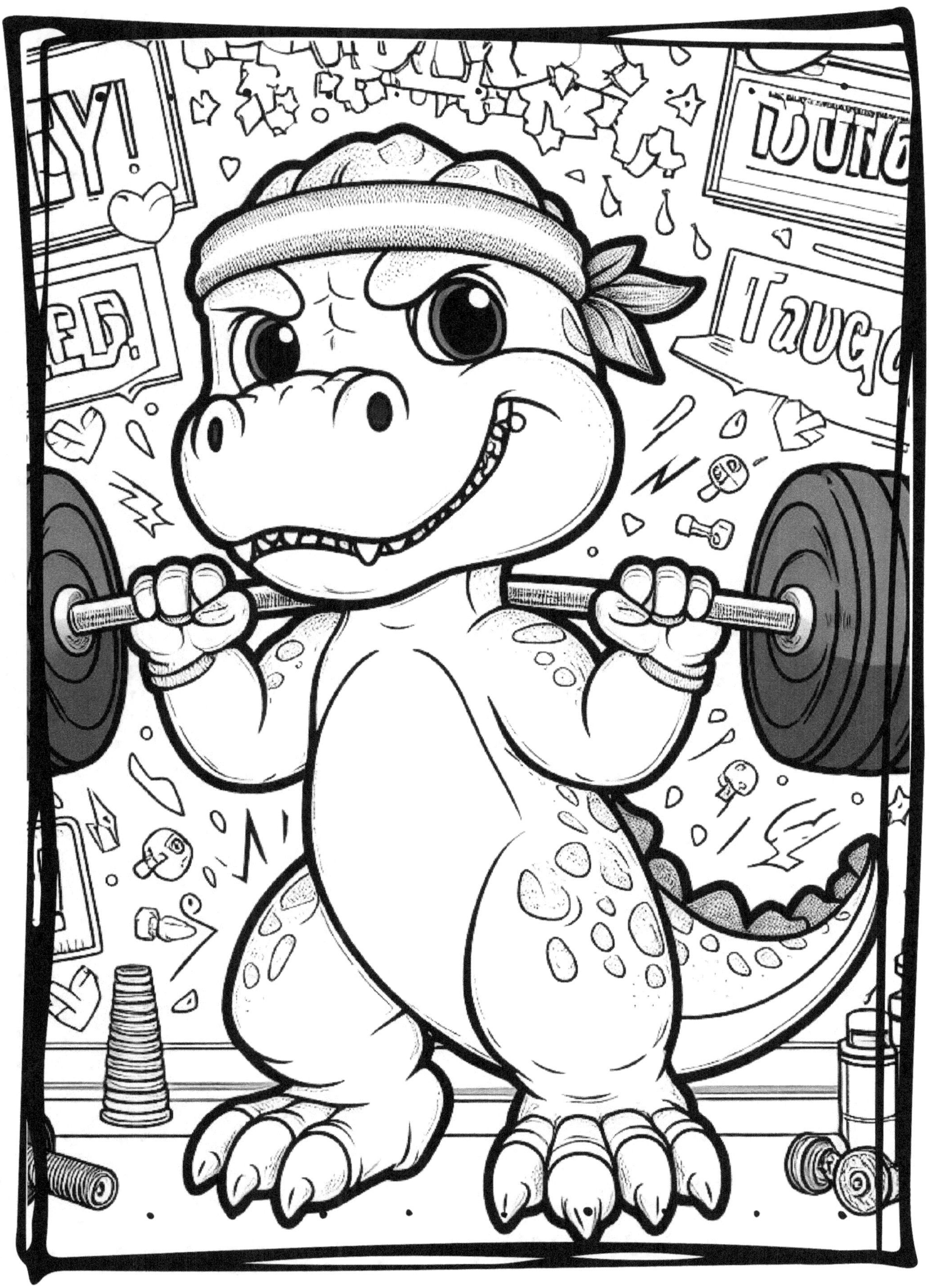

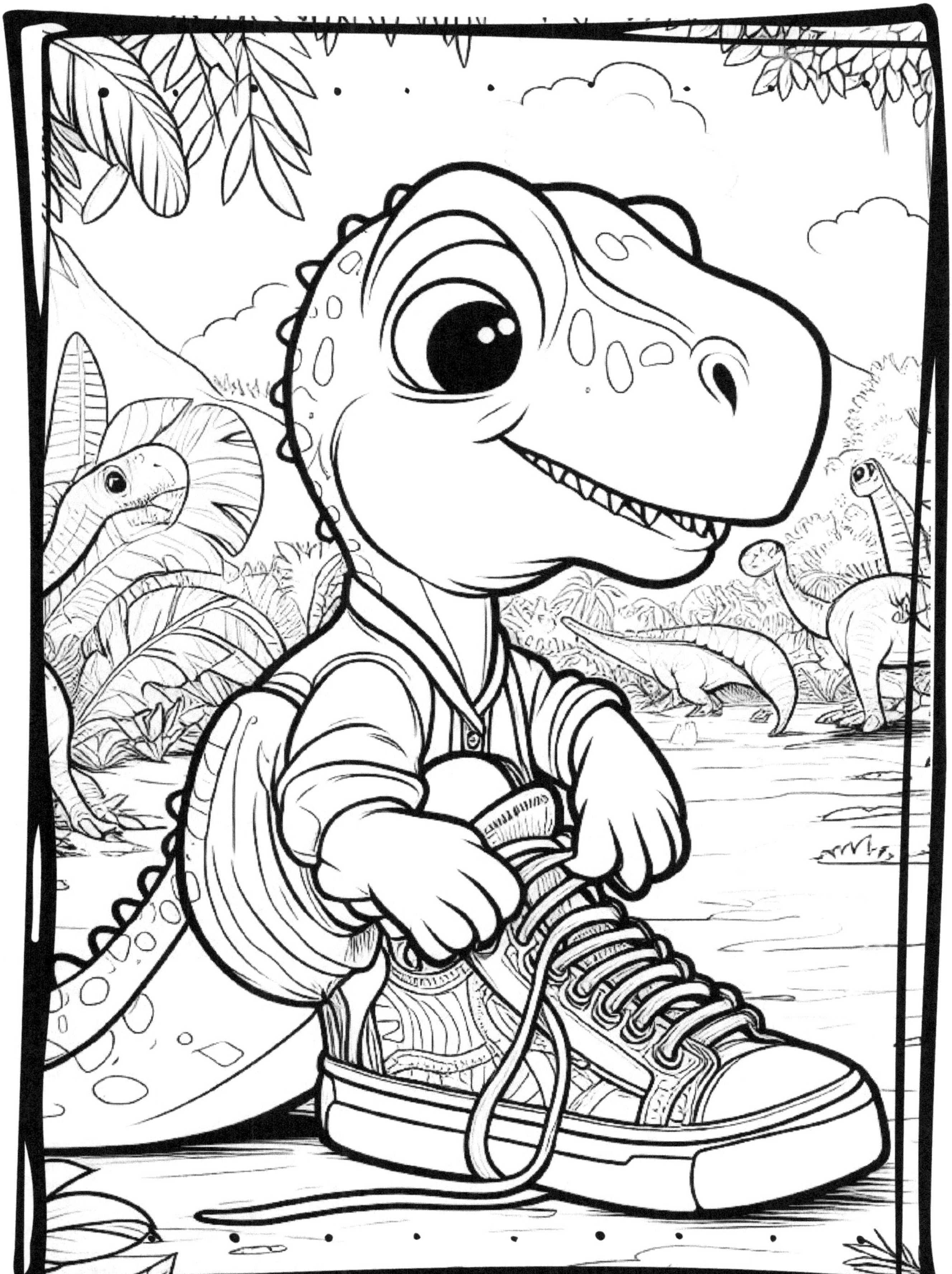

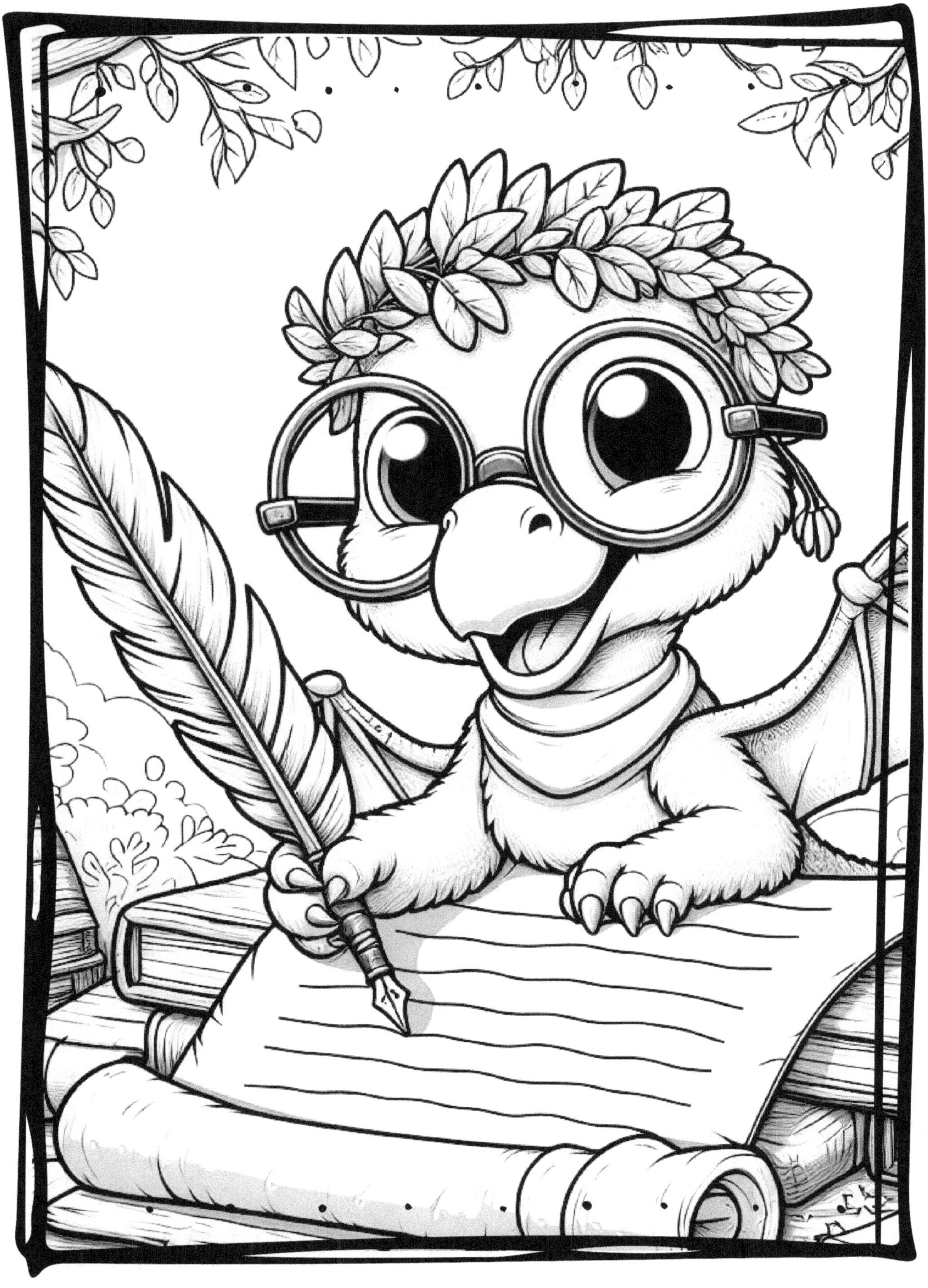

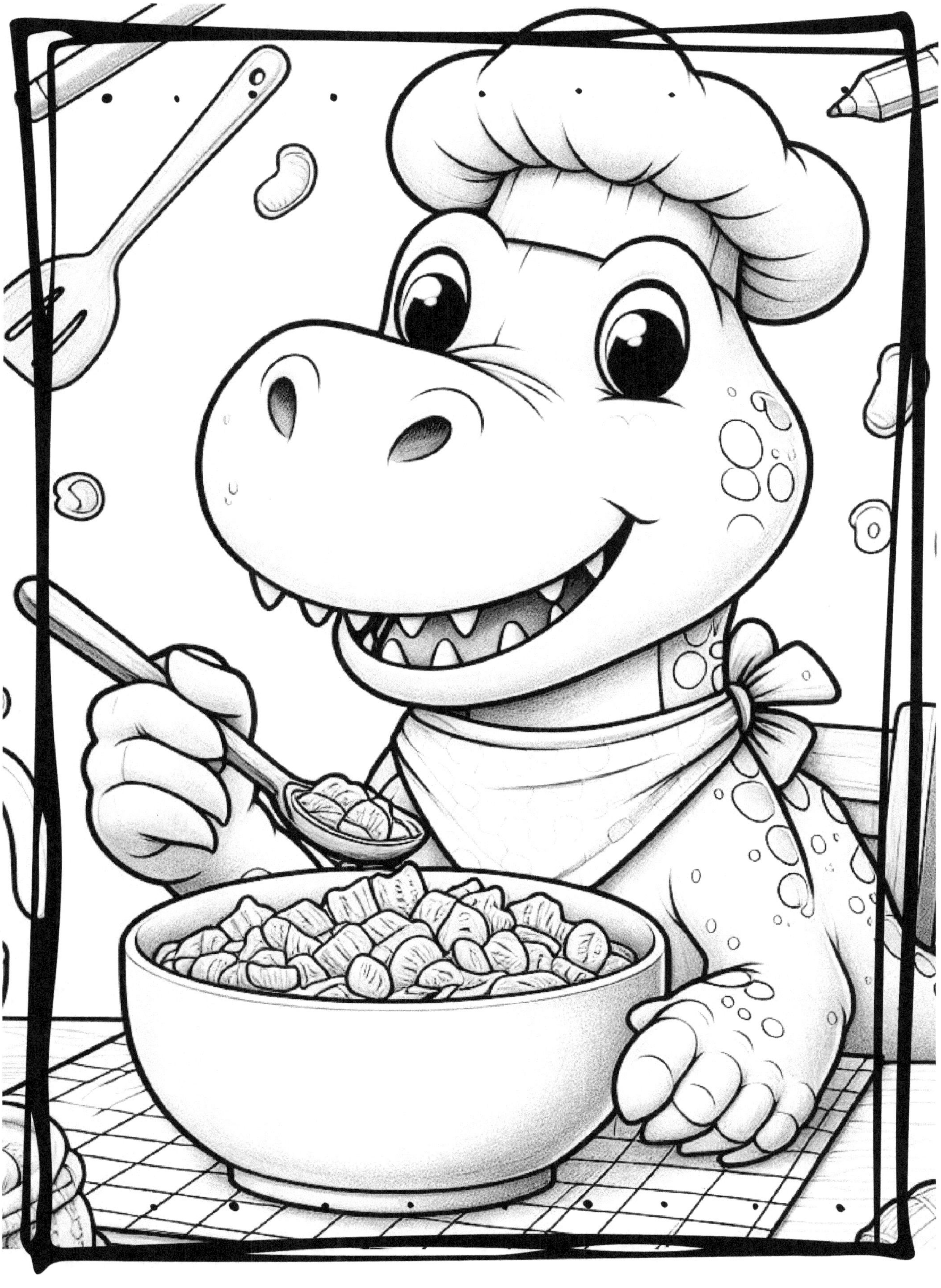

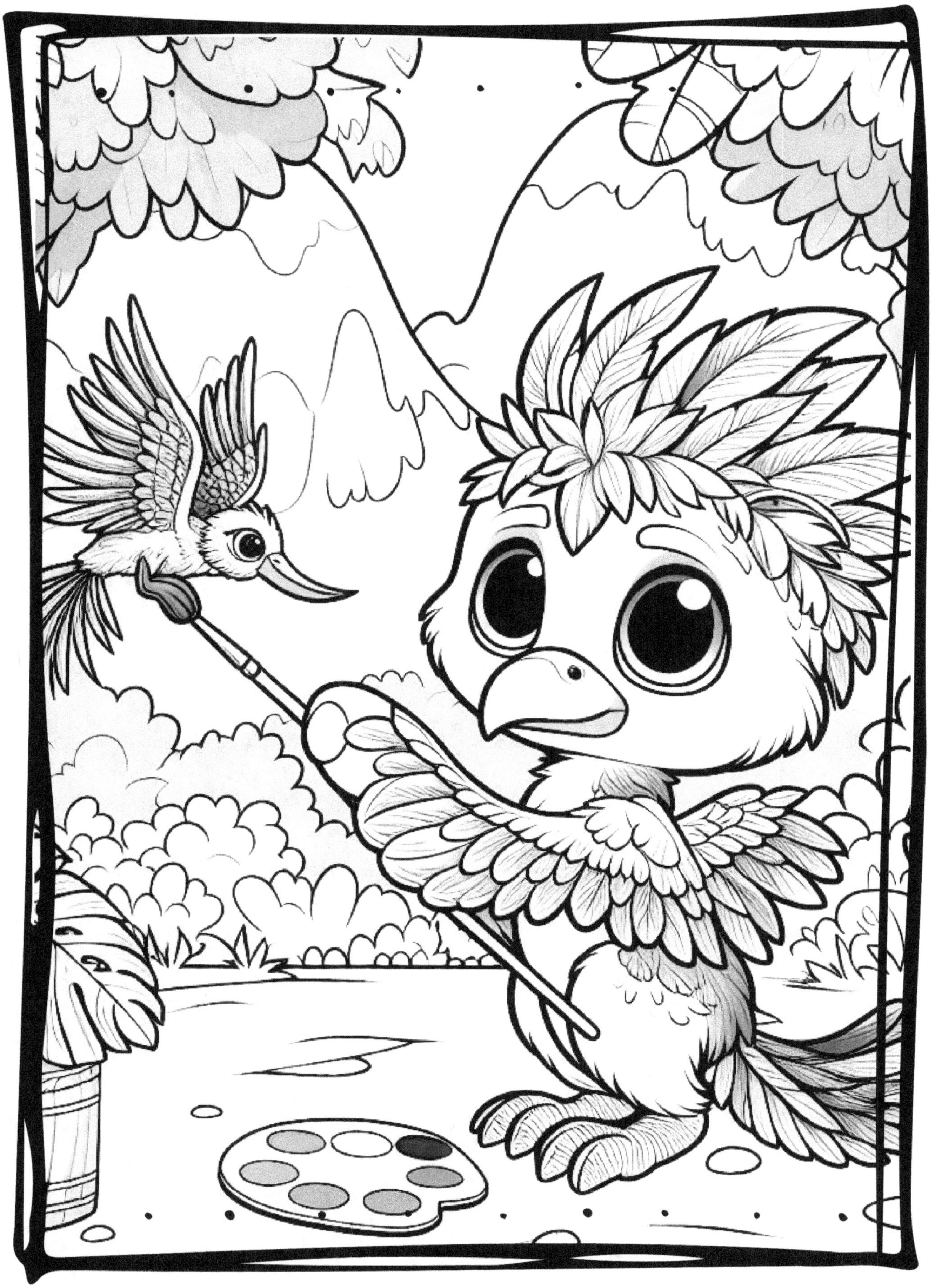

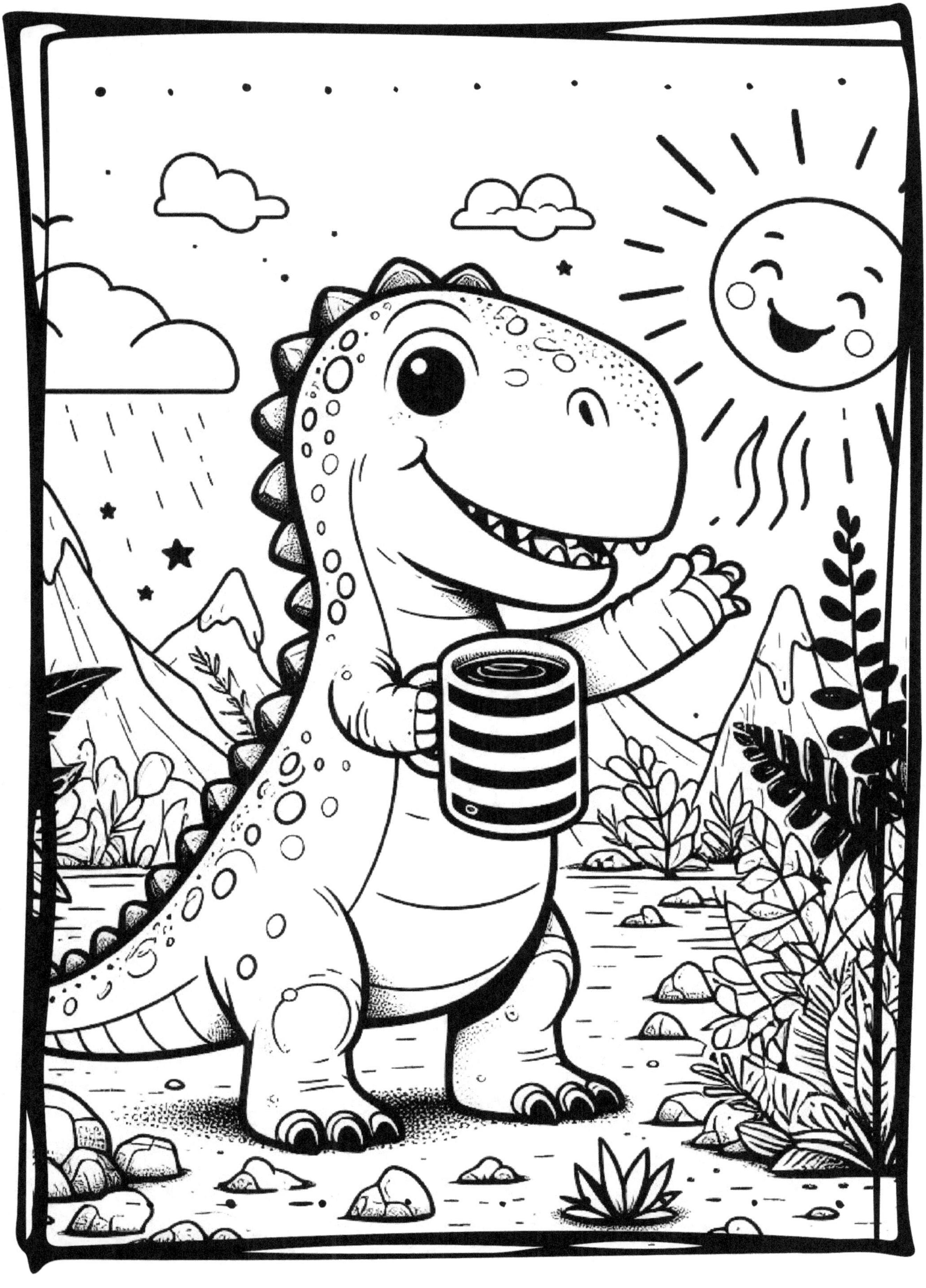

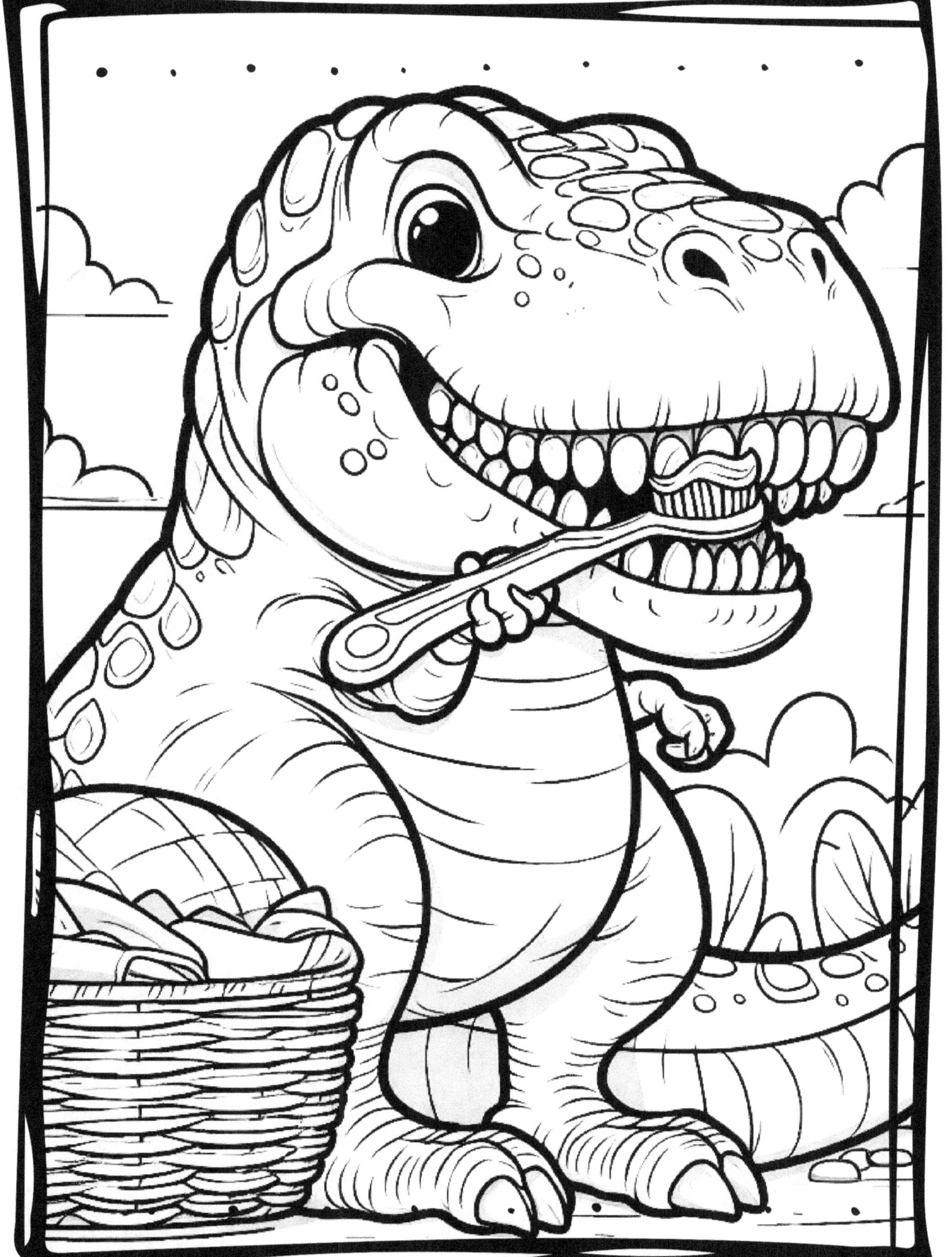

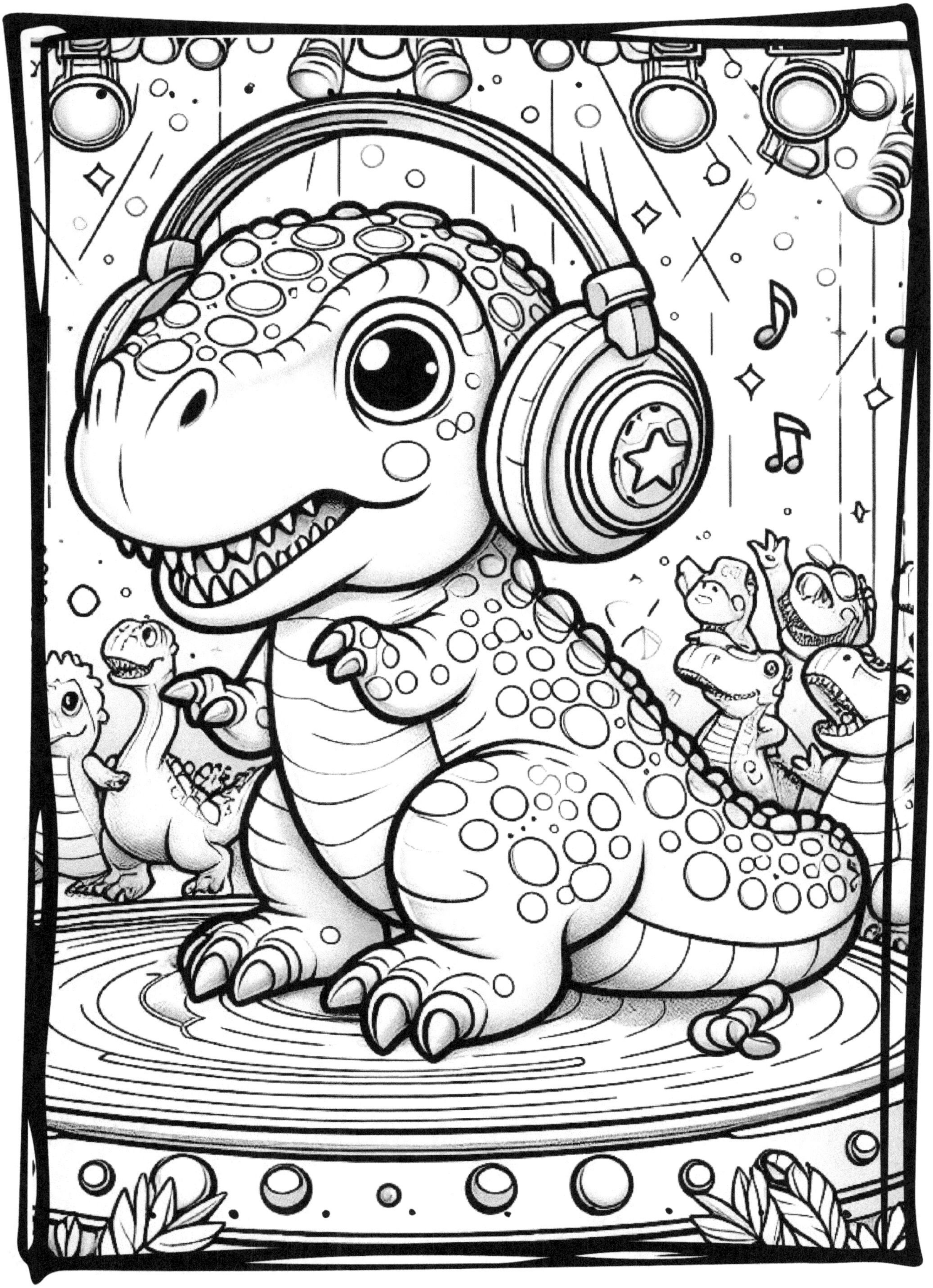

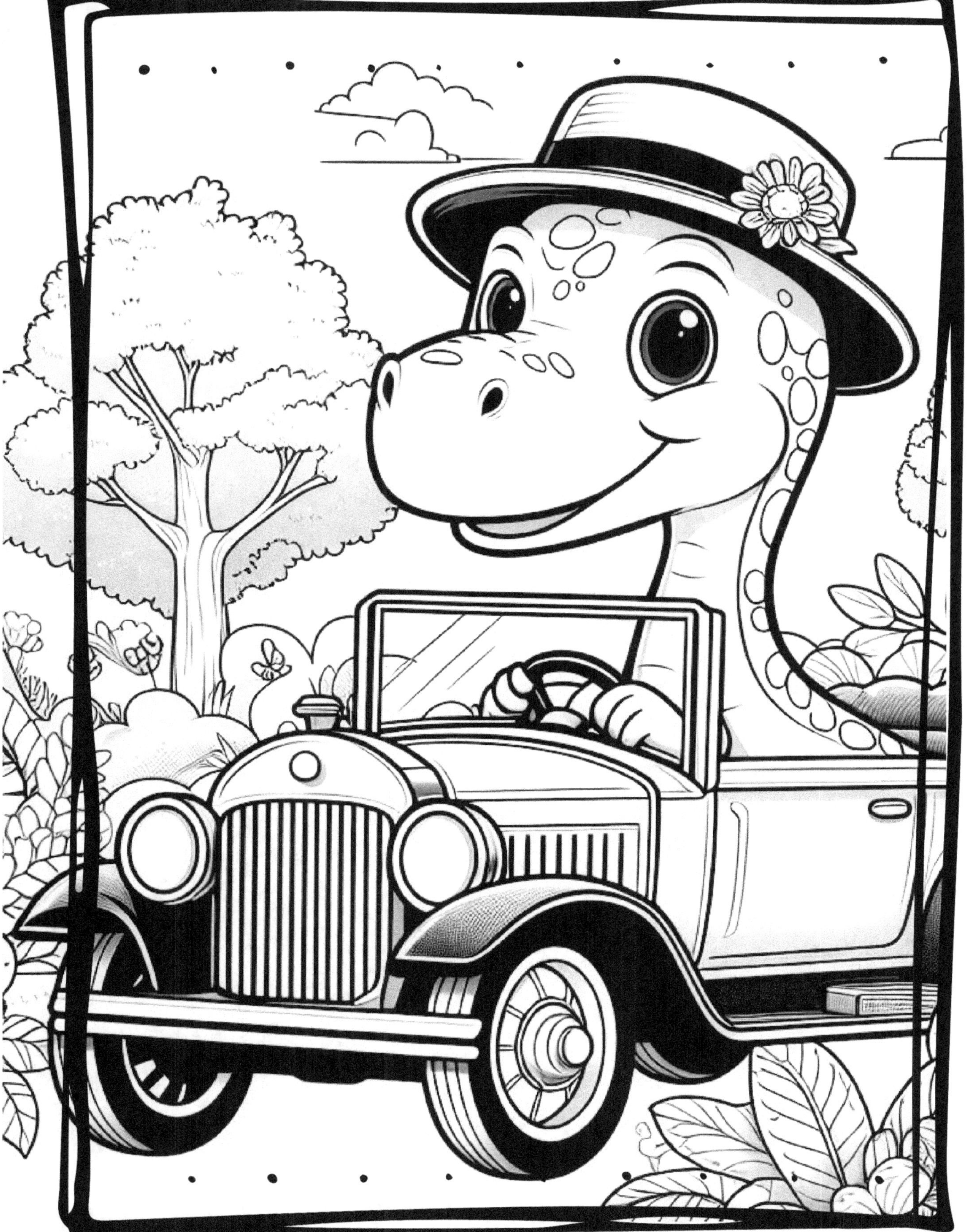

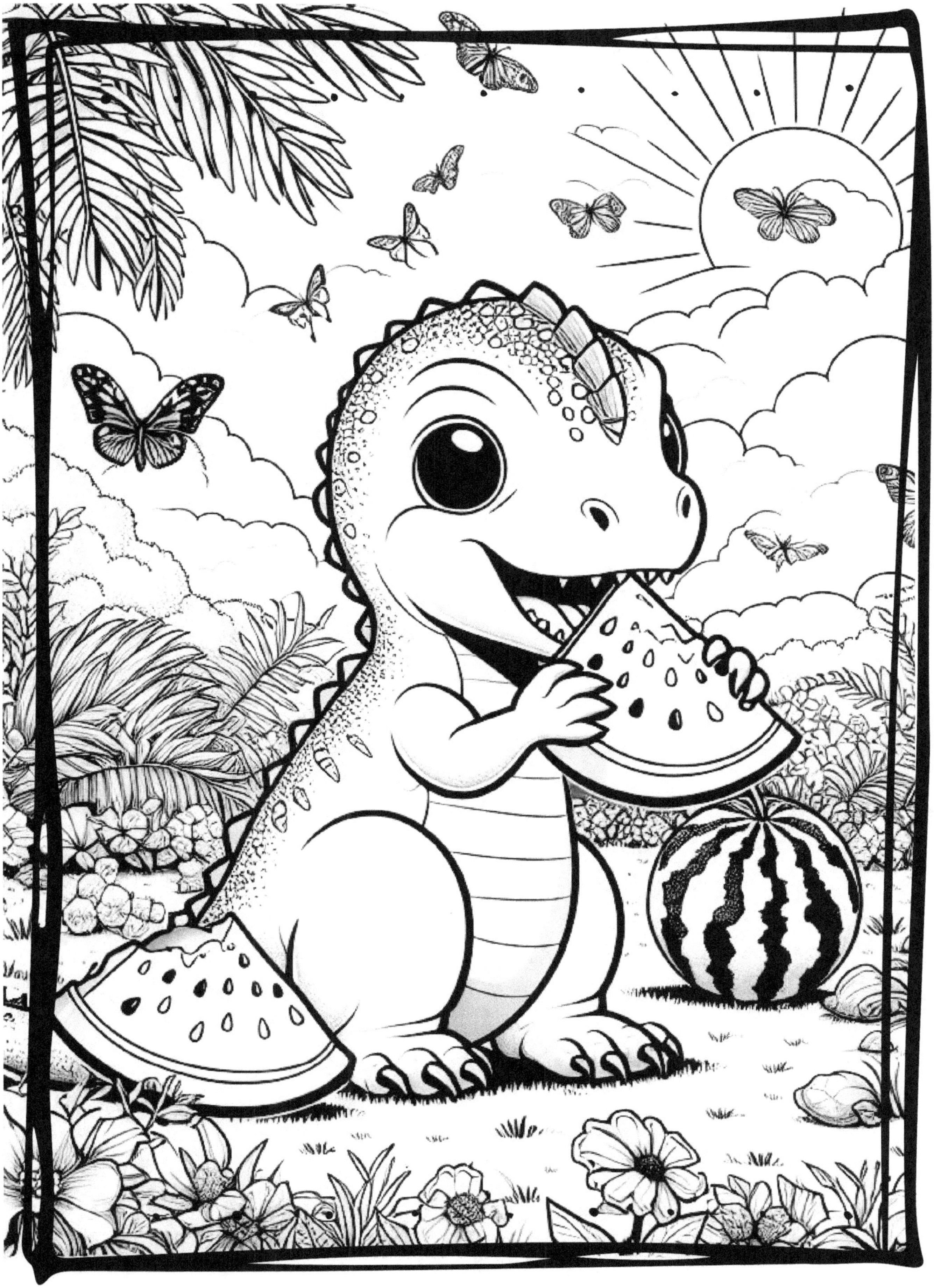

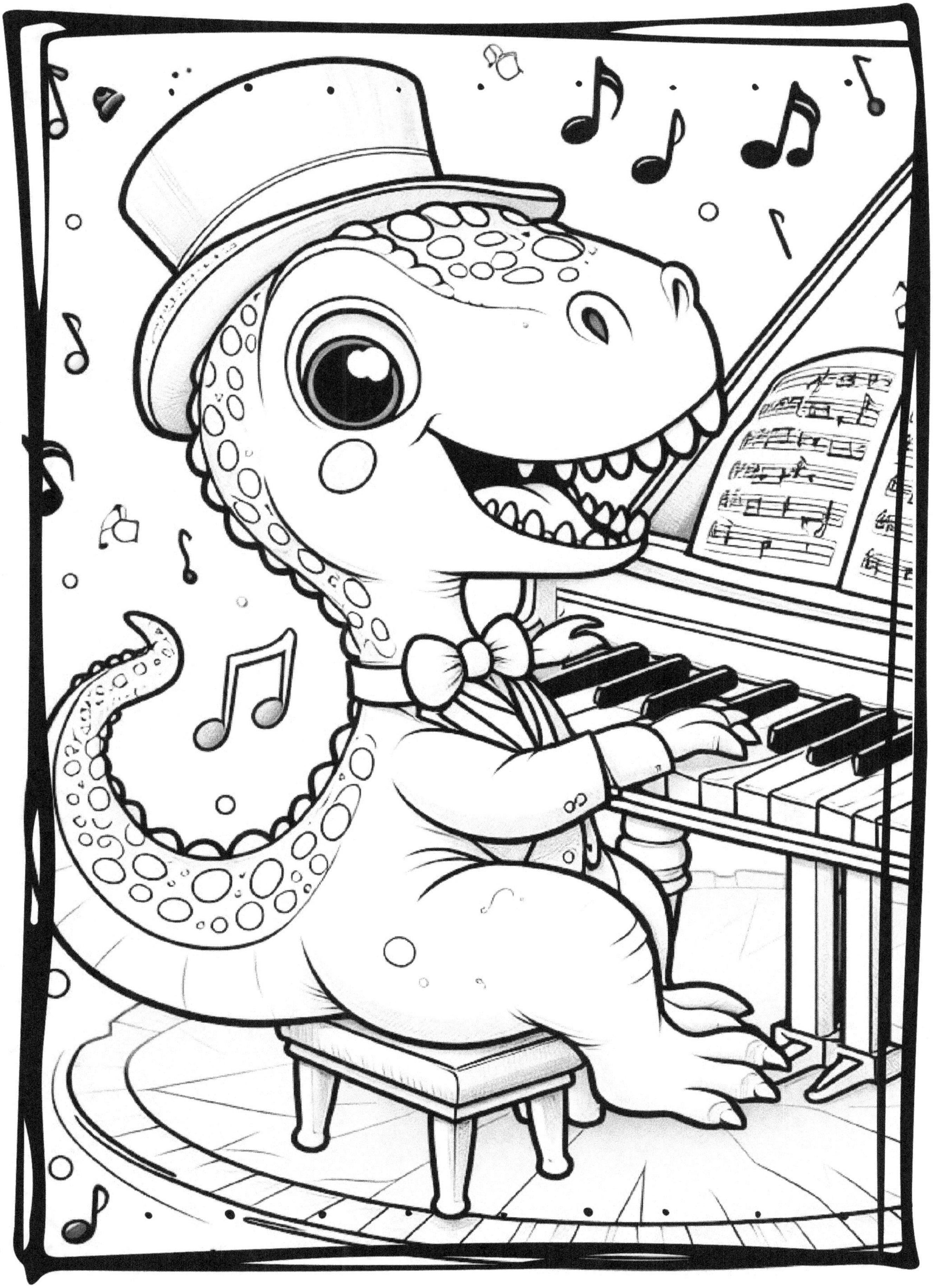

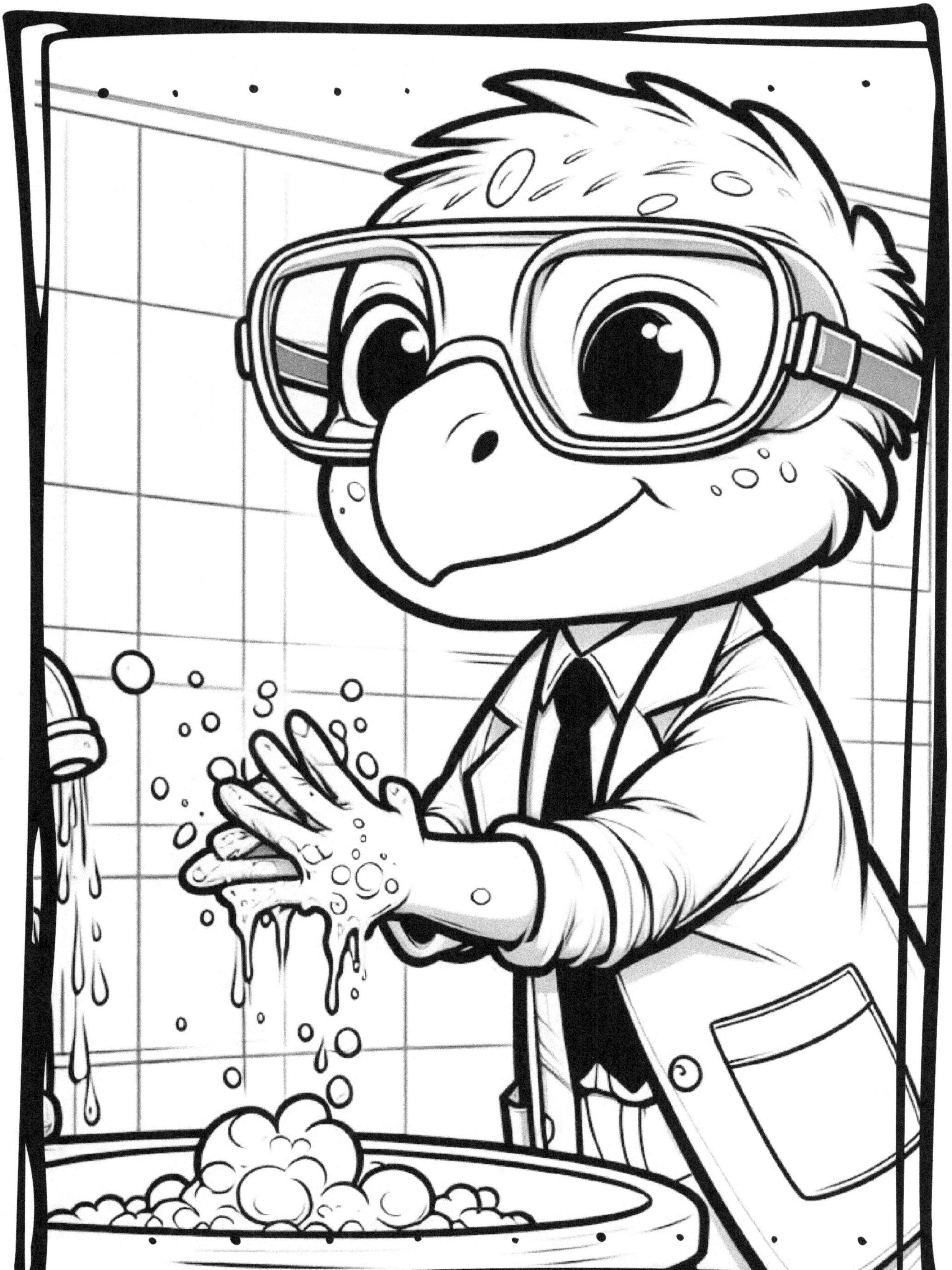

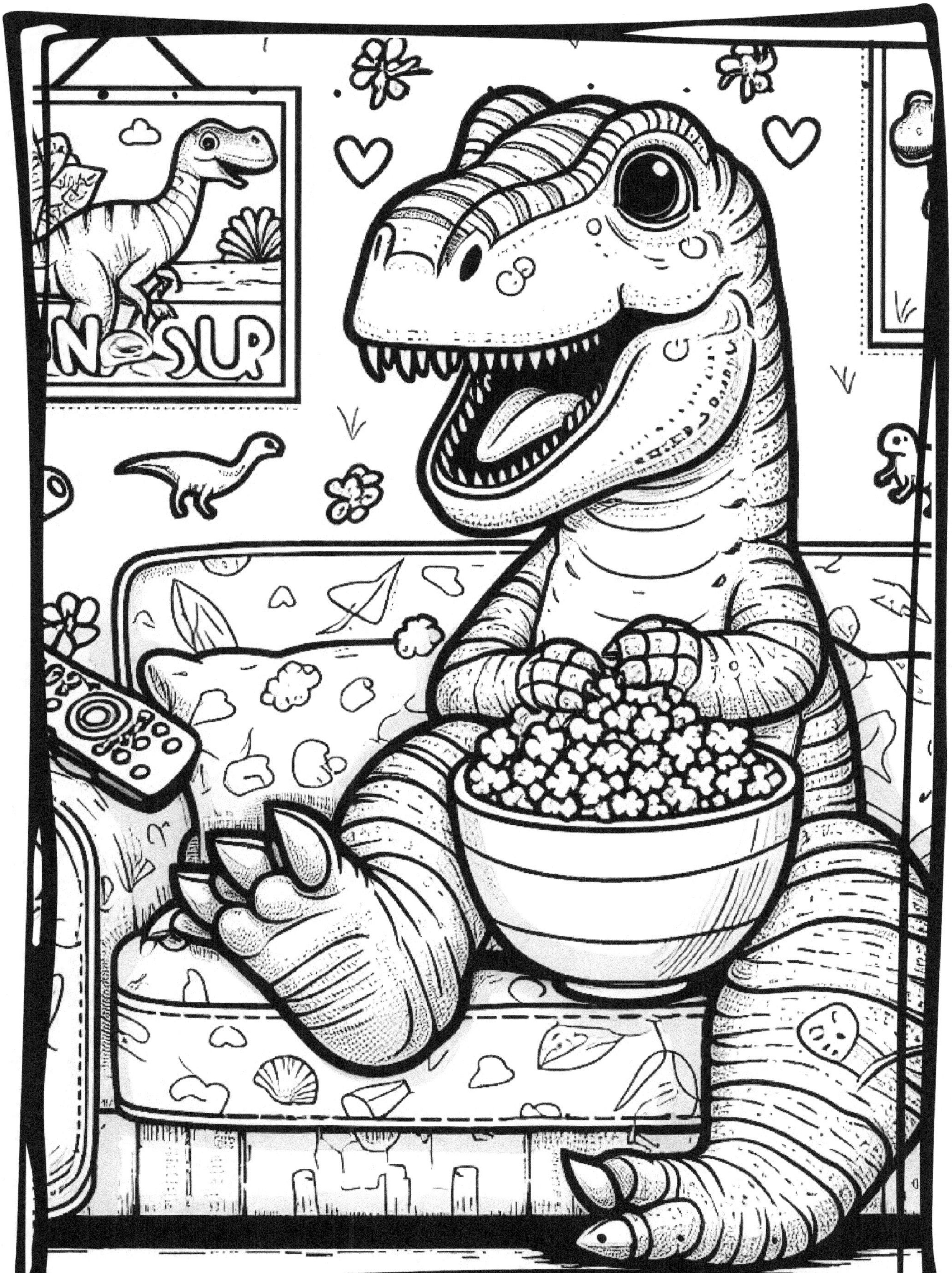

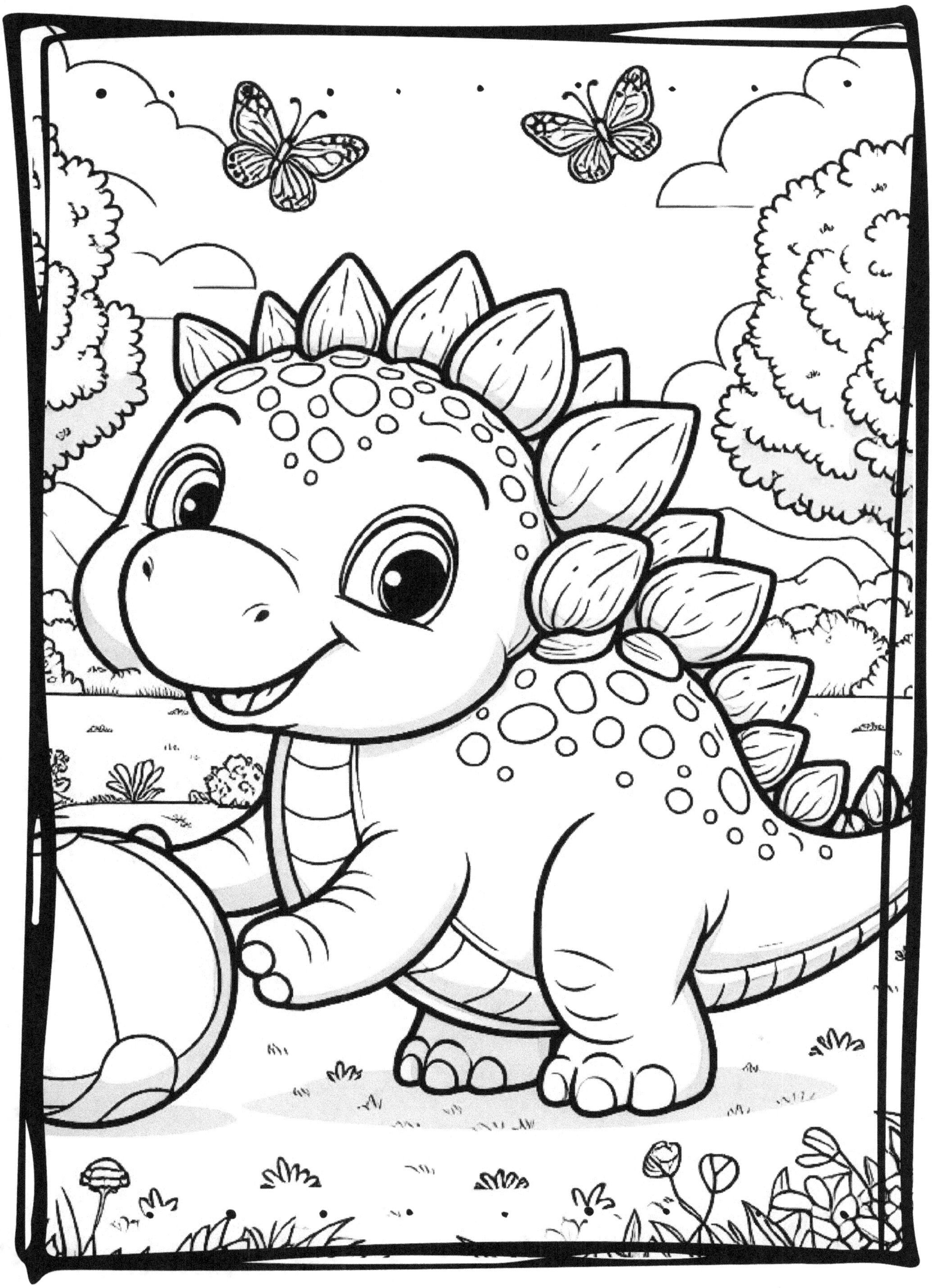

www.ingramcontent.com/pod-product-compliance
Lightning Source LLC
Chambersburg PA
CBHW082200290526
45794CB00008B/3371
9798870513317